# EXPERT PROI

## VOLUME 9

Conversations with Influencers & Innovators

# EXPERT PROFILES
## VOLUME 9

Conversations with Influencers & Innovators

Featuring

Michelle Foss-Zampino

Nick Elkins

Tricia Prues

Philipp Lomboy

Matthew Unger

# Copyright © 2019 Authority Media Publishing

Published by Authority Media Publishing Houston, TX

ISBN-13: 978-1-946694-27-0

Royalties from the Retail Sales of "Expert Profiles" are donated to Global Autism Project

## AUTISM KNOWS **NO BORDERS;**
FORTUNATELY NEITHER DO WE.®

Global Autism Project 501(c)3, is a nonprofit organization which provides training to local individuals in evidence-based practices for individuals with autism.

Global Autism Project believes that every child has the ability to learn and their potential should not be limited by geographical bounds.

The Global Autism Project seeks to eliminate the disparity in service provision seen around the world by providing high-quality training to individuals providing services in their local community. This training is made sustainable through regular training trips and contiguous remote training.

You can learn more about Global Autism Project by visiting GlobalAutismProject.org.

# Table of Contents

# Energetic Healing for Burnt Out Professionals, Practitioners and Caregivers

Michelle Foss-Zampino's father died the year she turned 40. She was just two years younger than he was when he had his first heart attack. She knew she was living a life that was leading her down the same dangerous path. Yet losing her dad, as painful as it was, showed her the choice before her: Let life happen to her or make her life happen.

Not long after her father's passing, Michelle signed up for a holistic practitioner course at Spa Tech Institute in Ipswich, Massachusetts. There, she learned about the powerful energy-clearing system called "Realizing Your Sublime Energies" (RYSE™).

She began doing RYSE™ exercises daily to prevent practitioner burnout. For the first time in a long time,

Michelle started to feel good physically, mentally, emotionally and spiritually.

In 2005, Michelle founded Healing Creative in Salem, Massachusetts to provide professionals, caregivers and practitioners an oasis from the stressors of everyday life. Today, Healing Creative has evolved into a wellness collaborative offering advanced holistic therapies, classes and nutritional products throughout Boston's North Shore and beyond.

Michelle is one of the first practitioners nationwide to teach groups and individuals RYSE™ for self-care, as well as teach wellness practitioners how to use RYSE™ for clients experiencing burnout and pain.

# Conversation with Michelle Foss-Zampino, Healing Creative

*How do you help your clients, Michelle?*

**Michelle Foss-Zampino:** Most people are suffering from some level of adrenal fatigue—a constant state of being in fight or flight mode—and it can take a catastrophic toll on your body. If you're experiencing chronic exhaustion, weakened immunity, sleep disturbances, food cravings, and/or pain, then you may be showing signs of adrenal fatigue. I help professionals, practitioners and caregivers reduce or eliminate chronic pain, experience greater peace and increase their vitality using holistic therapies.

When I started Healing Creative, I envisioned an oasis for your soul. We have a "no-judgment, meet you where you are" approach to healing. I wanted it to be a place where people could release the stresses of daily life. Clients can have an hour or an hour and a half just for themselves. Whether it is soothing a crick in their neck or needing a shoulder to cry on or experiencing a gentle touch to help them feel better—that was, and still is, at the heart of Healing Creative.

Today, the vision has expanded from only offering individual sessions to being able to help more people. We are able to do that by collaborating with other holistic practitioners at our studio spaces in Salem and Beverly, Massachusetts, as well as by offering group programs. My background is in massage and energy work, but I know that for some people, massage or energy work just isn't for them. Maybe they love yoga or acupuncture. That's why I've created a place where people can try different modalities like Qigong, yoga, Reiki or even wellness products. This is a safe place to learn about and explore holistic health, and how it can nurture and support you in your day to day life.

My vision for the next five to 10 years is to see and facilitate greater collaboration between the holistic and medical models of health care. While the medical model offers important technical, physical, and chemical health solutions, I believe holistic therapies offer the personal, emotional, spiritual, and energetic touch missing from traditional medicine. Through a collaboration, we can better serve our clients/patients to find their paths to healing, empowering them to be part of their own healing process.

*What inspired you to start Healing Creative?*

**Michelle Foss-Zampino:** From the time I could talk, I would tell people I wanted to be a doctor. My parents owned an insurance agency and hoped that I would come into the agency full time when I finished college. Having worked part-time in their agency since I was 12, I let go of my dream to be a doctor and started my career in the insurance agency after graduating college.

I worked my way up through the industry and, by 2001, I was an insurance executive. Then 9/11 happened, and it became increasingly difficult to do a "good job" due to the circumstances in the industry. Rates were skyrocketing and no one was happy. The underwriters, clients, producers, and agency owners were miserable. Suddenly, my successful career was spinning out of control as I found myself working way too many hours and living on sugar, caffeine, Advil, and Tums.

I had no idea the toll my career was having on my physical, mental, and emotional well-being. I always put others first. I always caved on my boundaries. I worked hard and played harder. And when I felt stressed, or unhappy, I would soothe myself with food, wine, and late nights of live music.

After 17 years in corporate, and a life-changing trip to Senegal, West Africa, I finally quit my job. I wasn't sure what I was going to do, especially since traditional medicine wasn't calling me anymore. But when a volunteer offered to do an energy massage for my dad during one of his hospitalizations, I was curious. If an "energy massage," whatever that meant, could help my dad find some comfort, then why not? As the practitioner worked, I watched my dad's pain melt away and witnessed a restful sleep envelope him. The practitioner told me he learned this technique at the Spa Tech Institute.

After my father passed away, I signed up for the holistic practitioner course at Spa Tech Institute, which is where I learned the powerful energy-clearing system called "Realizing Your Sublime Energies" (RYSE™) and began practicing it for myself. I became a licensed massage therapist (LMT), Reiki master (RM), Polarity practitioner, prenatal-perinatal massage therapist and certified educator of infant massage (CEIM).

Healing Creative evolved in 2014 from a solo practice into a collaborative of wellness professionals, offering a variety of holistic therapies, classes and nutritional products to help our clients become more energetically aligned and make sound decisions for their well-being. I've since become one of the first practitioners trained by Spa Tech Institute and RYSE™ founder Nancy Risley to deliver RYSE™ sessions to individuals and groups, as well as teach others to do RYSE™ on others in their practice or workplace.

*What is the biggest problem that you specialize in solving?*

**Michelle Foss-Zampino:** My practice addresses physical, emotional and/or spiritual pain. That might be helping a client with physical movement by doing massage to help a tight muscle release, or helping clients approach life in a happier, more joyful way by doing an energy session that calms and soothes their spirit. That's my goal, to alleviate pain in whatever way it shows up.

Some of my youngest clients are in grade school and some of my oldest clients are in their eighties. They're all telling me that there's this sense of being overwhelmed, whether it's coming from the exam that they're studying for, a deadline for a job, or they're worried about aging and their health. There's this global sense of overwhelm that is prevalent in so many areas of society today.

Being able to understand and manage those feelings so that you don't get overwhelmed, so that you can manage your life a little bit more effectively and joyously is powerful. I recently asked a young woman, "Where do you find your joy?" She shrugged her shoulders and said, "I don't know." She is only in her 20s. I remember having a lot of joy in my 20s, but more and more people seem to have lost that now. If we have no joy, why are we here?

*What is RYSE™ and how does that help alleviate pain?*

**Michelle Foss-Zampino:** RYSE™ stands for "Realizing Your Sublime Energies" and I started doing it as part of my curricula at Spa Tech Institute. It became a self-care practice that helped me to regain my own health physically, spiritually, and emotionally. After spending 17 years in the insurance industry and suffering significant family losses in my life, RYSE™ helped me focus on healing and feeling good.

As I have evolved as a practitioner, what I understand is that we are a system of circuits and wires–endocrine, nervous, and muscular systems. Our nerves are the wires that run through all those systems, creating the network that information travels on. When there is a disconnection in that system, people are going to experience pain. They may experience it on a physical level or a mental or spiritual level.

RYSE™ teaches people about their energy system and how it works so they can address an issue preemptively. For example, if you're engaging with somebody and it doesn't feel good, you can learn through doing RYSE™ exercises to become clearer about your choices.

One choice may be that yes, you can continue to engage with someone, knowing how to protect yourself so that you don't unwillingly take on whatever it is they're trying to give you.

Another choice is not to engage with that situation and walk away, doing it in a healthy, positive manner. RYSE™ teaches us a deeper understanding of ourselves and how we can manage our own systems so that we stay healthier and happier on a day-to-day basis. I do it every day for five or 10 minutes in the morning when I get up and it sets the stage for my day; then at various times throughout the day to check in on how my system is doing.

*What makes RYSE™ effective?*

**Michelle Foss-Zampino:** RYSE™ addresses the metaphysical and the physical, and it's backed by science. Our body's systems, whether the nervous system, the endocrine system, or the energetic system, all work together to provide us our health. RYSE™ gives us tools that we can bring into our day-to-day life that address body, mind and spirit.

RYSE™ also can work in conjunction with traditional healing and medicine. It helps bring another level of clarity so people can process through challenges quicker. I would not say do RYSE™ instead of traditional healing. I would say do RYSE™ in addition to whatever you're doing through your medicine.

We are evolving and still learning what works for our bodies and what doesn't. RYSE™ can bring us a level of clarity as to what does and doesn't work. I'm not going to tell somebody who's got some serious emotional issues to not continue to see their psychologist or their therapist. However, RYSE™ might bring them another level of clarity that they can process through whatever it is they're working on quicker and more effectively so that they can live their life with joy and vitality. RYSE™ helps you embrace your life force.

*What are some of the outcomes that your clients have experienced or achieved after using RYSE™?*

**Michelle Foss-Zampino:** One of my clients is a writer, sculptor and attorney. Being an attorney is his career, but he is a creative artist at heart. For the last four or five years he's been saying, "I really would like to get my work out there. I have all of these sculptures in the basement. I have these reams and reams of notebooks of poetry and stories that I've written. I'd really like to get out there, but I just can't seem to get out of my own way and it's not anything that's going to make me any money anyway, so I just need to keep doing what I'm doing."

He started doing RYSE™ with me three years ago. Since then, he's won numerous awards for his sculptures because they're not sitting in the basement anymore. He's actually putting them in art shows and getting awards. One of his books is just about ready to go to a publisher. He's actually manifesting the things that he wanted but felt he couldn't have. Whatever was holding him back, whatever was getting in the way of his full potential, has been alleviated. He has clarity, focus and a path to get his work out there and fulfill a dream that he's had for 50 years.

I have another client who has suffered with chronic shoulder pain. She has been a massage client for almost 15 years. Then she did one RYSE™ session with me. The shoulder pain is gone and has not come back. RYSE™ removed the core issue of whatever was creating her shoulder pain.

A new client has gone through a series of challenging emotional situations and hadn't eaten for two weeks.

After our first session, he left my office and immediately invited his sister out to lunch. Whatever was blocking him and keeping him in a dark place got released.

*What are some of the myths or fears that hold people back from introducing RYSE™ into their lives or into the workplace?*

**Michelle Foss-Zampino:** For businesses and organizations, and often with individuals, it's about showing them the tangible results. That's the challenge, because it is a relatively new modality that Nancy Risley created just 30 years ago. The results are happening every day in my studio with one-on-one clients and my groups, so it's about having the language to communicate those tangible results.

There is science behind RYSE™ that can engage the intellectual mind, so moving people through the doubts and fears often becomes about communicating in a way that doesn't sound mythical and magical. Professionals and organizations generally want positive impact on performance, which is a positive impact on bottom line. That's the corporate mentality. I can't say that's a wrong mentality because if the corporations are not making money, then they don't exist. What I'm inviting is that when businesses and corporations invest in creating a healthier and more supportive environment for their employees, individual and organizational performance increases.

When you have a happy, healthy environment to work in, you have happy, healthy employees that are going to want to show up. They're going to want to do a good job. That, in and of itself, will increase their bottom line.

*What's the most important thing executives should consider when it comes to creating that environment?*

**Michelle Foss-Zampino:** Most people are not only processing and dealing with their own emotions, but they're also engaging in taking on other people's stuff; especially in the workplace. If you're not mindful about that, it creates this environment of mess and murk.

Personally, I like to work in a healthier environment where it's light and bright, where I can think clearly and can come up with creative solutions to issues. I want to enjoy my work and the environment that I'm working in. What RYSE™ can do is help organizations and individuals create the most productive environment. If everyone is practicing RYSE™, they don't bring that negative stuff to the table.

Being mindful about our behaviors and how we interact with each other is powerful. If you've had a bad morning and you go into a meeting with your team, your manners and speech are likely to come from that negative perspective. If you've had a nice morning, maybe you get to the meeting 10 minutes early, you have five minutes to breathe and then you can step into that place of engaging with your staff. That's approaching your work and your colleagues from a different place.

When you practice RYSE™, you are more intentional. You are responsive to conditions; not reactive. You can engage positively even when you experience a challenging situation.

In 30 seconds, you can scan your system, release what's not serving you, and get yourself into a good place so that you can engage with your team or your coworkers, or with your family and friends, in a healthy and positive manner.

*It sounds like one of the bigger benefits of RYSE™ is that it has a ripple effect on the whole environment or group?*

**Michelle Foss-Zampino:** Yes. When everyone is doing their RYSE™ exercises and keeping themselves in a good place, oftentimes they will entrain to the lighter and brighter energy even when someone has a bad day. You can quickly clear negativity and clutter so that you can have a better day moving forward.

*How do you deliver RYSE™ to your clients?*

**Michelle Foss-Zampino:** I have a program called Experience RYSE™, which is a series of four live group meditations on a weekly basis either in the studio or at a workplace.

Normally, I will do the RYSE™ work on them while they're listening to singing bowls and a guided meditation. I do the RYSE™ clearing on them so they experience what it feels like to have a squeaky-clean energy system. Often through that experience, they understand how it feels in their own body and oftentimes that is the catalyst for them to want to learn how to do it for themselves.

I have another program that teaches them how to do that. It's called "RYSE™ For You": a 16-hour class where

I teach clients how to perceive their energy system, what is affecting it, and how to clear issues using specific RYSE™ exercises they can do on a daily basis that can take seconds to keep themselves in that good place.

I am also certified as a RYSE™ teacher trainer, which means I can teach a doctor, nurse, another holistic practitioner or someone in the corporate world how to become a RYSE™ practitioner so that they can do that in their own environment.

*What is the most common mistake healing practitioners and caregivers make?*

**Michelle Foss-Zampino:** We try to heal people by giving away our energy. We can't heal anyone if we're giving everything away. Whether you are holistic healers, doctors, nurses, teachers or caregivers, you are engaging with people through an exchange of energy. But, if we continually give our energy away, there is nothing left for us or anyone else. This often leaves healers feeling resentful and angry.

I see a lot of resentment and anger in society because we're drained. Many of us make that mistake. You think you can help, but then all of a sudden you're tapped out. You look to see who can refill you and there isn't anyone around. Then you're not in a good place to do anything including your job.

If it happens to be healing someone, it's not going to work very well. Or, you're going to keep giving until you can't even do your job anymore. Our planet needs healing. People need to have that engagement and it needs to come from a really happy and positive place; not a place of resentment and anger.

RYSE™ is an amazing practice that you can start today. Just take 10 to 30 seconds a day to close your eyes and take a nice deep breath. Feel what that feels like in your body. This sounds basic but it's an amazing place to start because it gives you that moment of peace and silence. All you have to do in that moment is breathe. People actually forget to stop and consciously breathe.

You cannot give what you don't have. If you don't have peace in your heart, you can't give peace. If you don't have hope in your life, you can't give hope. And if you don't have love for yourself, you can't give love. So, a good place to start is to just breathe and recognize those things in yourself, because then you can share them with others.

# About Michelle Foss-Zampino

Michelle Foss-Zampino is the founder of Healing Creative, a wellness collaborative offering advanced holistic therapies, classes and nutritional products throughout Boston's North Shore and beyond. Michelle is known for helping caregivers and professionals achieve optimal health, happiness, and wholeness using a breakthrough energy-clearing system called Realizing Your Sublime Energies (RYSE™).

She has been nominated for Northshore Magazine's Best of North Shore Awards, as well as been featured in Boston Voyager and Business Innovators Magazine. Trained by Spa Tech Institute and RYSE™ founder Nancy Risley, Michelle is one of the first practitioners nationwide to teach groups and individuals RYSE™ for self-care. She's the only RYSE™ practitioner on the

North Shore of Massachusetts, besides Nancy, who can teach practitioners how to use RYSE™ for clients.

Additionally, Michelle is a licensed massage therapist (LMT), Reiki master (RM), Polarity practitioner, prenatal-perinatal massage therapist and certified educator of infant massage (CEIM). In her spare time, Michelle is also a professional vocalist and performs with the award-winning West African pop band MAMADOU.

**WEBSITE**
HealingCreative.com

**EMAIL**
michelle@healingcreative.com

**LOCATION**
Salem and Beverly, Massachusetts

**FACEBOOK**
Facebook.com/HealingCreative

# Relieve Financial Stress with Your Spouse by Going Beyond Budgeting

If you're experiencing stress in your relationship, you're not alone. While the reasons will vary from couple to couple, the American Psychological Association's "Stress in America" survey found that 31% of adults with partners attribute money as a major source of conflict in their relationship.

Another survey by Suntrust had similar findings in that 35% of people they polled blamed finances for the stress in their relationship.

For many couples the first step to taking control begins with establishing a budget. But personal finance coach Nick Elkins says that a budget is only a Band-Aid unless you look beyond the numbers on your spreadsheet.

In this interview, Nick reveals some common misconceptions and important considerations around budgeting. He also shares how you can approach the subject of finances with your spouse to increase the likelihood of long-term success.

# Conversation with Nick Elkins of Family Finance Freedom, LLC

*How did you get your start as a personal finance coach?*

**Nick Elkins:** I earned a bachelor's in finance and I thought that meant that I knew everything. And of course when you know everything, you tend to fall flat on your face. And I did that for many, many years with personal finance decisions. My wife and I constantly joke that the reason we're so good with it now is because we were 10 times worse back then.

And that's one of those things where personal finance is more than 80% behavior. It's not all knowledge. I knew a lot and still made a lot of mistakes. And what I realized over time is that my background in education and being able to have conversations with people and really listen and ask good questions helped me to explain complex information in an easy to understand way. And for me, that was a clear sign that I needed to make this my business, my way of serving people in the world.

*Are you primarily focused on helping clients to change their behavior with their finances?*

**Nick Elkins:** Yes, absolutely. There are so many free resources out there that help you with the what and the how. I help them focus on the why and put a strategy in place that helps them avoid the common pitfalls that have plagued them in the past, including their own behavior. There are obviously times where I want to reach through my computer and just kind of put my hand on either shoulder and shake them...and there are times where I am pleasantly surprised by a decision they made.

What I do is help my clients figure out how to live the life that they want with their money, how to set goals, how to create a plan to reach those goals, and then how to actually take action against that plan. And so that is behavior change, right? Because everybody knows you're supposed to set goals, but how many people actually do set goals as an adult until they realize what the power of setting those goals is.

*How would you describe the people that choose to work with you?*

**Nick Elkins:** You'd be somewhat surprised that the people I work with are seeking out the help of a financial coach. Most people see the type of people my clients are and say that person must be really successful, that person has it all together. They've got the beautiful house with the white picket fence, the two cars, the three kids, and the dog. But internally, that person is wondering how they're going to put Christmas gifts under the Christmas tree this year. Or they're wondering how they're going to pay for soccer this season.

So the group that I work with have combined household income of $100,000 or more. And at the end of the day, these people, even though they've crossed this really emotional threshold of making over $100,000, at the end of the day, they don't feel like they have anything to show for it. They're not making progress. Or they get to

30, 35, 40 years old and they say, "I make $150,000 a year and I have nothing saved for retirement. Why is that? What now?" Those are the people that I work with and I help them figure out what's causing that and then set a course for where they want to be.

*Are they in that situation because they're trying to keep up with the Joneses?*

**Nick Elkins:** I would say that's one of the many challenges, and it goes a lot deeper than just keeping up with the Joneses. It goes into a cultural mindset of that's what we're taught. That's what we're ingrained with. Even my kids who are seven, five and three, notice when there's a logo on their shirt and there's a kid in the class who doesn't have a logo on their shirt or vice-versa, and they wonder why that is. They wonder why somebody has a dirty shirt and why theirs is always clean or why another kid's parents pull up in a McLaren and I'm driving a Honda Accord and they wonder why Daddy doesn't have the cool car.

So, it starts really early because the status symbols that our society has put in. If you're the type of person that's motivated by that status, then keeping up with the Joneses is a really big obstacle to overcome towards financial freedom. But...it CAN be done!

*It must be even more difficult to stay on track when you have so many outside pressures that are influencing your financial decisions.*

**Nick Elkins:** It is. And that's one of the reasons behind the idea of "values-based personal finance." If one of your values is keeping up with the Joneses and showing off your status symbols, then absolutely you should be spending your money towards that. You know what I mean?

If you're running a business and you need to look the part, then yeah, you probably should be wearing a pretty nice suit. You should probably should be driving a car that's not going to get you laughed at when you pull up. Right?

But you could have a conversation with your spouse and say, "Honestly, I really don't care about all that. We've been trying to impress people that we don't even like. We're trying to impress people with this big house that we don't even want to invite over to our house. Why?"

If that's the case, which is with MOST people if they really stop and ask themselves, then what has happened is you've actually been spending according to "drift," which is the opposite of intentionality.

You're not aligning your money and your expenses with what you truly value in life. And so that's what I work with on my clients is to get really clear with them about what they actually find important.

*Is it important for you and your clients to have these deeper, values-based conversations early on?*

**Nick Elkins:** That's not one of the initial conversations that we have as a coaching relationship. I'd be shooting myself in the foot and frankly I would not be doing them a service if we had that conversation right off the bat. Because most people that reach out are looking for a little bit of help with budgeting. Or they're trying to figure out how to pay down their debt more quickly. Or "Should I put $5,000 in my 401k at work or should I use it in an emergency fund?" But yes, we absolutely have deeper, values-based conversations. Once we get the immediate, urgent items triaged, then we can focus on what's truly important to them.

*What are some of the myths and misconceptions around budgeting?*

**Nick Elkins:** For years and years, when I heard the word "budget", it meant we were poor. We can't have that. It's not in the budget. Well you can't have that. We're not going out to dinner with your friends because it's not in the budget. You wear the Payless shoes instead of the hundred dollar Adidas because of the budget.

You hear that painted enough times - and of course, you know, all your parents are trying to do is not spend money that they don't have. But what they've done is they've unintentionally created this monster in the closet called the budget.

And so, there are so many people out there who are afraid of that word because the very nature of the word makes them feel restricted. And, and so for me, if a client is apprehensive about the word budget, it's because they don't truly understand what a budget is. It doesn't HAVE to be restrictive or suffocating. It doesn't have to tell you what you CAN'T do. A budget is there to tell you what you CAN do.

*How do you explain budgeting so that your clients see it as a positive tool?*

**Nick Elkins:** So, the way that I look at a budget is – let's say I have a friend in Los Angeles. And I'm in Tampa, Florida. If I wanted to drive from Tampa to LA, I can look at a roadmap, right? So, a budget is a roadmap. When you Google the word "budget" or "personal budget," something like 1.6 billion results come up. And the very first one you're going to find is a spreadsheet image that has a bunch of expenses, separated by month.

It has nothing to do with your goals. It has nothing to do with when your money is actually coming in. It is extremely intimidating. The way that the traditional person thinks about budgeting and the way that the schools taught it for such a long time is essentially like me sitting in Tampa and going, "Well, I want to get see my friend, but I don't know what city he's in, so I'm just going to start driving. Oh, and I'm going to drive in reverse by looking through the rear-view mirror," because I'm only basing my budget on past expenses. There's a chance that I could get to my friend's house. It's pretty darn low though, right?

But that analogy carries over in the idea of what a budget truly is. If I want to see my friend, then I know that I need to get to LA, right? So I have a destination in mind for where I'm going. So that's one of the first things that you need to have with the budget. You need to have a clear goal, a clear vision for what the future is, whether it's near term or long term, and of why you're budgeting. What are you budgeting for? What goals do you have to get to that point?

The beauty of a budget is personal finance is so personal, right? So, for some, a budget is like saying, "I'm just going to hop on Interstate 10 and take it across the country and get to LA as fast as I possibly can." That's one way. And that would be the way that a lot of people think of budget typically works, which is go as lean as possible. Don't spend. Don't step foot in a restaurant unless you're washing the dishes. Right? I mean we've all heard that advice on personal finance radio.

But I believe a well-formed budget is just like a road-map. I have the option of making a pit stop in Louisiana or Houston or Arizona and I can visit friends and family along the way. Or I can see the sights. Or I can go out of the way and I can visit somebody or something along the way. And for me, that means you're allowing your budget to take you to places that you set as goals while still maintaining a level of focus on your long-term goal as well. If you use your budget to plan ahead and earmark money for a specific purpose, then it gives you the option of doing those things.

*What's the best way for a couple to start on their budget?*

**Nick Elkins:** The best way to START a budget is by looking backwards. The best predictor of future performance is past performance. So, you want to know what to put in your budget, look backwards for the last three to six months and categorize all of your expenses from your bank account. Find out what the average is and take into consideration any of the outliers.

For example, Christmas gifts tend to pop up in November and December so you're going to spend a lot more money those months.

So, figure out what your average spending is and that is that your starting point. Because if I say, "You're a family of six and that means that you shouldn't be spending more than a thousand dollars a month on groceries," for some people that's going to work and other people are going to laugh at me, you know? We're never going to talk again because it's unrealistic and I've lost them. We must keep an eye on the fact that personal finance is PERSONAL.

When a finance coach or expert tells you what that benchmark is that you should be targeting, it's often not taking into account where you live. It's not taking into account your goals or your lifestyle. For all I know you eat out at in and out Burger five nights a week, right? Or you could be a family that is 100% vegetarian, which is going to be a lot less expensive because you're not paying for meat. Or you're the type of family that buys only organic grass fed beef.

So there are many different things in the budget that have to be personal and have to be based on what you're used to spending as a starting point.

Now, once you truly understand where you're at, that's where you start looking into the future and you start looking and saying, "You know what? In order to meet that goal, I need to find $400 in the budget. Well, let me go through my subscriptions. Oh, look at this. I haven't even opened Spotify in the last three months. I don't need to be paying $20 a month for a Spotify account."

Obviously if you're overspending $1,000 a month, then yes, definitely cut expenses. But I would say only cut expenses once you've identified what those goals are. If you don't have goals specifically, then cutting for the sake of cutting is going to open the door for you to take on new dedicated expenses, and that's going to make it even more difficult for you to make progress once you are committed to this.

*How important is it to have your spouse on the same page when you put a budget together?*

**Nick Elkins:** When I talked about my own family's personal finance journey, I mentioned how many mistakes we made. I said "we" but for the most part it was me making those mistakes. I have had clients look at the way that I used to manage my finances and more than one has said, "Man, your wife must've thought you were a huge prick."

Yes, that was one way to manage finances. But it's not a way to manage a marriage. The way that I handled things and the way that a lot of people I see are handling things with finances - it's not a team-based approach.

We found ourselves in that place simply because my wife doesn't like math and doesn't like money and didn't want to have to deal with the personal finances. So, I managed it.

But of course, then I was making decisions about what she was allowed to spend and what she wasn't on money that she was working for and it didn't work. Getting on the same page with your spouse is paramount to the success.

Having deep, intimate conversations about finances isn't easy though. That's why a lot of my clients come to me because having someone else there who understands the goal, but doesn't have an emotional tie to the conversation can really help in clearly communicating.

*It must be difficult when one spouse has to be "the bad guy" with the finances.*

**Nick Elkins:** That's entirely true. The analogy I use there is those three-legged races that we used to run in school and camp where my right leg is tied to your left leg. Imagine you're standing there at the start line of a three-legged race with your spouse and you have no idea where the finish line is. You think it's off to the left at 10 o'clock and your wife thinks it's off to the right at two o'clock.

You guys are going to fall. You're going to continuously trip over yourself and you're going to get frustrated at each other because you can clearly see the finish line is at 10 o'clock and she's sitting there going, "No. It's at two o'clock," and you're not communicating well and you're getting frustrated.

That's the way that so many of my clients come to me. They're having these arguments about finances where it's not even a finance issue. It's a communication issue because the budget is not doing its job. It hasn't been set up properly. When they take the time to clearly identify where their finish line is and how they're going to work together to get there, they can get there SO much faster.

*How do you know that your clients are ready to talk about underlying issues and values?*

**Nick Elkins:** it generally comes naturally to me to know when someone is ready for a deeper level conversation. Typically, it's one spouse who thinks that they know everything about finances and the other one doesn't want to know, doesn't want to be involved, or just doesn't care.

And when that uninvolved person starts getting involved or starts engaging in the conversations in a meaningful way, now all of a sudden, the spouse who's been all about budgeting for the last three years before they came to me, now all of a sudden that person is put on their heels and almost surprised because the spouse is now engaging. That is a perfect time to have a deeper level conversation because you've got a person who thought they knew everything on their heels, and you've got a person who was disengaged, who now has engaged.

*What do you do in situations where one spouse isn't engaging in the process at all?*

**Nick Elkins:** I've had clients where one of the spouses says they're engaged and then goes and does the opposite. I can see in their budgeting software that there's some kind of rampant spending that's not according to what the budget says. That person will typically say that they're engaged and say that they want to make a difference, but they don't actually believe it themselves. Right? So, having those conversations is really, really difficult. And obviously if you have a spouse that is that way, you know how difficult these conversations are.

For me, that's where I don't even make it about money. It's more about communication. It's about goals and dreams and visions for the future. It's about the "why." You know, like Simon Sinek, "Let's start with why." It's about, "Why are we doing this? Why are we having this conversation?" and getting to the purpose of this whole thing. Because if the spouse doesn't want to have to deal with it at all and is unwilling to approach it, it's a lot more difficult for the marriage to survive.

Typically, they're not saying that they don't want to be involved because they're not invested in the marriage. They're saying that they don't want to be involved because of a past communication issue. Maybe they got involved and they let their guard down, but then they felt targeted or cut off at the knees. So now they're protecting themselves.

*How do you juggle the mechanics of personal finance with the emotional challenges a couple might need to overcome to make progress?*

**Nick Elkins:** That's a good delineation. I would say that if we get to point in our working relationship where it's obvious that deeper level, more emotional conversations need to be had in order to be successful, then we've built that trust. We've built that relationship and that rapport that they're almost expecting me to help with that.

Once they get the tactics down on the finances, they're excited to dive into the deeper level stuff because it's one thing to put a Band-Aid on your finances by getting a new budget in place.

And I think that's a great thing. But it's another thing to have meaningful conversations about deep-seeded issues that you learned from your parents growing up and that your spouse learned from their parents, and they could be in complete opposition to each other.

Having those meaningful conversations naturally happens, especially with context laid. Because we can easily refer to a previous conversation we had. Or we can go to a specific line item in their budget and use that as the example of, "Here's what we're talking about this for, because it affects this thing." And so having that context and having that tie into how it's going to affect them to have that meaningful conversation, people are actually willing to go there more often than you'd realize.

*Can a proper budget and personal finance plan really help a couple reduce their stress?*

**Nick Elkins:** It ABSOLUTELY can. A lot of time, the clarity of just knowing where everything is going eases you. The stress often comes in because you don't even know what you're spending all your money on. Being able to see everything clearly and be proactive instead of reactive is so exciting.

My favorite client ever is married and had just had a baby. He was 31 or 32 years old at that time. He didn't budget at all. And his wife had a paper budget and they really didn't know how much money was going out every month. And they were having some arguments about finances. They just felt like they weren't really living a very purposeful life. That's the core of why they came to me. And through implementing a budget and having conversations, over the course of the last nine months, they paid off over $40,000 in debt. Both have gotten raises. And they're having conversations that they've never had before about what their future looks like and about potentially retiring before they each turned 50. And what kind of vacations they want to take.

Just last week, he messaged me, "Do you have time to talk?" So, we hop on a call and he rattled off a list of 30 cities that he and his wife talked about over dinner the night before and listed out places that they wanted to visit. They didn't even realize they wanted to travel because they didn't realize that it was possible for them.

As soon as they started putting things on paper and looking at it and saying, "We could do this!" now all of a sudden, a whole new world of possibility has opened up for them. And they're excited to budget now because it means that they get to take money from their paychecks and put it into their goals.

*How would you describe your role when you help a couple with their finances?*

**Nick Elkins:** You know how many professional athletes fail as a coach? Even some of the greatest players of all time. But they're not very good coaches. Right? It's because playing their sport often comes naturally to them. Yes, they really worked hard to own it, but all that talent came naturally to them. But how are you supposed to explain how to do something to somebody who's struggling and doesn't come naturally to them if everything comes naturally to you?

Some of the best coaches, though, are the ones who had to study technique and strategize just to hang in there with the good players. They had to overcome obstacles and are able to help others do the same.

It's both a blessing and a curse, obviously to have made so many mistakes. But I look at my ability to learn from my mistakes as a superpower. And with all of these mistakes that I've made, over time I realized friends and family were reaching out to me to ask how to handle certain situations because I've overcome many of the issues they're facing themselves.

One day I helped someone realize that he could save $15,000 by paying off his student loans early with money that he was wasting and didn't care about either way. And he asked me, "How much can I pay you for this?"

And my mind exploded at that moment because here I was thinking I've made all of these financial mistakes and I'm going to have to work until I'm 70 because we haven't gotten anything saved. But all of a sudden now somebody sees potential in this as a business opportunity for me. He didn't even realize that that's what that was. He was just being nice, "Hey, can I pay you?"

And so, I had that realization that this was an opportunity to combine all of those mistakes that I made with my fulfillment and happiness from having genuine, deep level conversations with people and getting to know them and help them. One of my clients told me the other day, "I don't even feel like I need your help with finances anymore, but I love talking to you because every time we talk I feel like you're rooting for me! I feel like I have somebody in my corner cheering me on, telling me that I'm going to make this happen." And that, to me, is such an honor to be able to take something that I've always taken for granted - that I just truly believe the best in people - and use that to help others.

*What would you tell someone that's skeptical about using a budget with their spouse?*

**Nick Elkins:** They should ask themselves if what they're currently doing is working. If it's not, if you feel like you're struggling, if you feel like you're frustrated, if you feel like your marriage could be better, if you could create financial intimacy, if you could have conversations with your spouse about money without getting frustrated and you're not doing any of that right now, it's probably time to try something new.

I would say it's not even just budgeting, right? It's budgeting in a specific way. It's budgeting from the time you get paid to the next time that you get paid. And looking at what does my money need to do for me between now and the next time that I get paid. It's not saying, "How much money am I going to make this month and how many expenses are gonna go out this month?" and hope that there's more income than there is expenses. Sure, that's a "budget." But that's not going to do you much good.

Another big myth about budgeting is a lot of people think that tracking is budgeting. "If I look at what I'm spending, then that's budgeting." That's a great first step because you have some awareness around what you're spending. That is fantastic and it will really serve you well as you get into budgeting.

But you're not budgeting yet. You're tracking. Budgeting is taking that information and aligning it to what your goals are and what your future is and then actually checking in with it as an accountability piece.

*What questions should a couple ask themselves as they look for someone to help with their budgeting and personal finances?*

**Nick Elkins:** Can this person actually get me to my goals? Has this person reached goals themselves? Is there a specific plan that they have? Can they articulate what that plan is? Can they tell you the process that you're going to walk through even beyond the technical aspects?

Again, there's a delineation between the technical part of budgeting and the behavioral part. If you're looking at a financial coach who doesn't have empathy or who isn't helpful and who doesn't enjoy having conversations, who isn't fun to talk to, there's another way. You don't have to go that route. Is the financial coach in your corner? Are they rooting for you? Do they believe that you're able to do this or are they only telling you that?

So, when you're looking for somebody to give you quality financial advice or guidance, make sure that you're not just a dollar amount to them. Make sure that they have the heart to walk you through this in a way that is meaningful for you.

# About Nick Elkins

Nick Elkins is a personal finance coach and founder of Family Finance Freedom, LLC.

**WEBSITE**
FamilyFinanceFreedom.com

**EMAIL**
nick@familyfinancefreedom.com

**LOCATION**
Tampa, FL

**FACEBOOK**
Facebook.com/FamilyFinanceFreedomLLC

TRICIA PRUES

# How to Make Content Marketing Manageable

A recent study by Kapost and Eloqua showed that content marketing had lower up-front costs and longer-term benefits as compared to paid advertising. Another study by demandmetric found that inbound content marketing costs 62% less than outbound marketing and generates 3x as many leads. These findings have caused businesses to shift their marketing from traditional advertising to content creation and distribution. But this transition can be challenging for busy entrepreneurs.

In this interview, Tricia Prues shares her insights on the value of content marketing, how to avoid common pitfalls, and how to effectively manage these processes and work requirements.

# Conversation with Tricia Prues

*How do you help coaches, consultants, and small business owners?*

**Tricia Prues:** I like to say that I take care of all the things that drive people nuts so that they don't have to do it. I'm not going to cook you breakfast, but when it comes to editing, content marketing, and getting information out to help your audience learn more about whatever product or service you're offering, I'm on it. Or just help people and get them more information to help their lives.

For editing, in terms of written content, just get your brilliant ideas down on paper, send them over to me, and I will help you clear it up and put your message out there the way you want it to be seen. You don't have to worry about cleaning it up and wonder how the sentences are supposed to go together. Just let me do that.

And helping with ideas. Sometimes people really aren't sure how to get information in front of their audience. There's this mental block of, "I don't know how to do this. I'm not good at writing. I'm not good at videos. I'm not good at X, Y, and Z." Well, you're a lot better than you think you are, and let's help you along the way, whatever that looks like.

*Why have more of your clients gravitated towards content marketing rather than to traditional forms of marketing, like advertising?*

**Tricia Prues:** It's where people are. You go to where people are. A lot of that looks like social media, newsletters, email lists, and blogs—people love subscribing to blogs. People love consuming information, and that's a really great avenue to take. We're just in a different generation of how we're marketing ourselves and how we're helping people, and there's so many different ways to do it when you're online.

*In what ways have you found content marketing to work more effectively than traditional advertising methods?*

**Tricia Prues:** Traditional methods can work. People talk about the "know, like, and trust factor." Before I want to buy from you, I want to know who you are, I want to like you, and I want to trust you. And once you provide me with valuable information, I'm more likely to look into your product and to consider what you have to offer me. So you'll see a lot of things in ads where people will be offering this really great information, and then they'll follow with the sale. And that's a really important thing to do: provide value. Once you've kind of warmed people up a little bit, then you can ease into a sale, as opposed to these huge billboards or ads saying, "Hey, come buy my stuff because it's really great."

*What are some things that people get wrong when they first start with content marketing?*

**Tricia Prues:** One is people have probably seen content marketing done poorly, decided they don't want to do it that way, and thought, "I don't even know if I want to mess with it."

Others think, "This person says to do it this way, and this other person says to do it this other way. I don't know what to do." So, people get stuck in the jumping phase rather than moving forward and putting something out there. Because while there are these wildly successful people who do it a certain way, that doesn't mean that that's the way that you have to do it. And that's just it—trying something out. And if it doesn't work after you gave it a fair go, just tweak and maybe see how some other people are doing it.

So, a lot of it is mental blocks that people have because they worry about, "What if it comes off as too salesy?" or, "I don't know how to do this." Sometimes it's just technical knowhow.

But people just want to do what they do well and don't want to mess with other stuff. It's just, it's a pain. Sometimes it's a matter of, "How do I share something on Facebook? How do I get it in front of people? What's a blog? What is website hosting? What are email lists?" There's nothing wrong with not knowing. We all start out in that place. And so, some of the technical knowhow is just some people will schedule social media posts, meaning you put things in this software program and it kind of does it for you. But they're asking, "What in the world is that? How am I going to figure out these different things?"

People have so much brilliant content, and they need to move towards getting it out there. At the end of the day, if we're in business, we want to have people pay us.

And kind of the first way to make your way into that is getting good information out there for people and moving from brilliant ideas to okay, marketing with these ideas and helping people learn how to help themselves.

*How do people get past their fears about the technology required for content marketing?*

**Tricia Prues:** Some people just don't want to do it, period. "I don't even want to think about it. I never want to try it. I don't want to bang my head up against the wall. Someone else can have it." Whereas other people start out doing it but later realize, "I'm putting more and more time into this thing, and I'm losing time not only for my business, but losing time for my family." I mean, a lot of us get into the entrepreneurial space because we want more time freedom. And that can happen sometimes.

Other times, not so much. And what can help with that time freedom is bringing someone onto your team. But sometimes it does take getting to that pain point where you recognize that you're having to compromise things that you really don't want to compromise.

And I think everybody hits that at a different time. Some people see it in the very beginning and can kind of let go of that control. Because for a lot of us, it's a control thing. Either I feel like I should do it all and I should be able to, or I just straight up don't trust people with my passwords. With, "They could make me look bad online." And there's just a lot of fears that people have. And I mean, they're legitimate fears. That's okay. And so, it's good to really get with somebody and move past those fears because they don't have to be as much of a hindrance.

*Is it fair to say that the shelf life of content market-*
*ing is longer than traditional methods? And if so, is that*
*a benefit?*

**Tricia Prues:** It's a double-edged sword. "What you
put out there is there forever!" and "Oh, man! What you
put out there is there forever." And that's true. If you're
putting out good quality content, that's great, and let's
all lean towards that. Right? And that's the amazing
thing about blogging and social media and different
things is it can extend and extend.

Sometimes we'll go into Facebook and say, "Wow,
this is an old post from three years ago." Well, what do
you know? Someone found it, and it's serving them at
that moment in time. Or, you Google something and this
blog post from eight years ago is still there because it's
helping people.

Same with YouTube. You may have experienced
searching in YouTube and you'll see "three days ago" or
"three and a half years ago." But if it's quality content,
it's going to serve people possibly for years and years.

*It sounds like content marketing can be a lot of*
*work. Are there ways to make it easier?*

**Tricia Prues:** The beautiful thing about the online
space is you can take one piece of content and do what's
called "repurposing." Say I do a video and I talk about
grooming dogs and people can watch the video. Great.
Well, from that one video I could do two weeks of social
media posts with little snippets from wisdom that came
from that video. Or I could do a blog post, or I could take

a Facebook video and move it over to YouTube. Then I could take that YouTube video and put it in an email to my subscriber list. You can take one piece of content and use it so many different ways. Maybe you take a compilation of YouTube videos and put it for sale.

That's the brilliance of technology and being able to use one piece of content in so many different ways. And the great thing with evergreen content—the things that aren't necessarily season-specific or something that's going on in politics or whatever it may be—is you could even space it out.

*Is there a danger of having duplicate copies of the same content on the Internet?*

**Tricia Prues:** You don't have to take one thing and vomit it everywhere on the Internet. You could say, "Hey, you know what? I think this might work well for a course I want to do in six to eight months." And chances are, unless someone's a super stalker, they're not going to be on every avenue seeing every single thing you're putting out there. And if they like it that much, then they're probably not gonna mind seeing things more here and there.

If you've built up enough trust (know, like, and trust factor), then they're going to say, "Okay, cool." Or they're going to say, "I don't really feel like looking at this," and maybe they'll come back in a few days.

Generally, if your audience loves you because you're serving them well, they're going to be loyal even if they see you post something in a few different ways. If it irritates them, they'll just take a break. Or if they go, then maybe you're not the best fit to provide for them anymore.

*What do you do if some people in your audience are turned off by this new approach?*

**Tricia Prues:** Sometimes we move on from the people we're learning from, and that's okay. I'm not always going to be able to serve people. I hope that I take someone to the point where they can move above and beyond. That's the goal in helping people: we want to elevate them. And when we elevate them, sometimes we just let them go, like, "Go! Blossom and flourish, young grasshopper!"

I don't want to be like, "Oh, I'm just so nice and I love people and I want to help people." But I have a heart to give and to serve and I want to respect where people are and honor where they are, then help them move forward. And if I can help someone get to the point where they feel confident doing something on their own, sweet.

Because if I'm going to keep trying to please people and please people, people can smell desperation a mile away. They know when we're like, "Oh no! Please don't go! Please keep paying me please!" I think there's a point at which things could get stale. And I want to be excited about what I'm doing. I want you to be excited about we're doing—what we're doing together. And then it may last a long time. It may not. There's an acceptance there. And I think that comes from having a healthy attitude of serving and giving, not necessarily being so focused on my success, but rather being focused on your success.

*What are the common mistakes that people experience when they start doing content marketing?*

**Tricia Prues:** One thing I have seen is people go, "Alright! I'm just going to give everything because I have so many brilliant ideas and I want to get them out there and it's going to be great!" And then they go, "Oh no! I have a week of things to help people, but then I have nothing else." Or maybe someone will think, "Alright, I'm going to post on Facebook. I'm going to start a blog. I'm going to do a newsletter. This is awesome. I'm going to help people, and it's going to be great." But when we give, give, give, we don't have much left.

People want things that are bite-size, too. A lot of us aren't going to read something that's 600–700 words, but we love 100-200 words. A 30-minute video? Eh. I'll watch a 2–3-minute video. Give me everything you've got in three minutes.

Another thing that people need to think about is how well—or not well—they're delivering it. There are some people—and I'm totally not judging here—who just don't get along with the English language very well. And that's okay, and you don't want that to hinder you when you're getting these brilliant ideas out there. And it's good to get help from somebody to kind of get started and then clean things up a little bit.

It doesn't mean you have to hire someone for $500 an hour to help you. It's just may be getting a little bit of help on board or having a friend read things over. It doesn't have to be paid. It's just allowing yourself to be vulnerable and ask for help because we may feel like we're an expert in this area, and so we should just be able to do it. And we're kind of worried about going, "Actually, I don't know that I feel really comfortable with this, so I should have someone help me, but I don't know if I want to. Does that make me look weak or ignorant or incapable?" And it doesn't. And you don't have to necessarily do it the right way when you get out there; just tweak things as you go along. Some people say, "I've gotta do it this way." Well, try it. If it doesn't work, try something else.

*Where do you suggest that people get ideas for topics for their content marketing?*

**Tricia Prues:** A lot of times it's starting where they are. Say you're really engaged on social media. Even posting on your personal Facebook profile, "Hey, I'm looking for some help with this," might get a slew of comments, and you go, "Wow! I didn't know that was possible!"

Or if you're in groups—I mean, there's so many people out there who want to help. And just by taking the step to ask for help, it opens up so many doors. When you're feeling insecure, there's an aspect of pride in there because we want to look good and feel good.

Letting that pride go and letting the insecurity go and just opening ourselves up opens so many doors because if people don't know that we need help, then they can't help us. And so many people want to help and see us succeed.

*Can content marketing work for people that have face-to-face, brick-and-mortar type businesses?*

**Tricia Prues:** Absolutely. I have one client that has had a bridal gown design brick and mortar business for many years. She wanted to get into the online space. But there there's so much out there to consume about how to do it and what approaches to take. She happened to see one of my posts in a Facebook group where I offered to help someone with their content marketing. She saw it and said, "Yes!" and put the little SOS emoji up there.

And she told me, "I just want to sew! I want to get into the online space and I want to help people, but I just want to sew and let somebody else do the other stuff."

She said, "I have these notebooks of ideas that I'll jot down." I told her to send them to me. I looked at her notes and wrote a blog post and put social media posts together. And after she read a couple of them she said, "Oh my gosh! I love how you write from my voice and you're helping this dream come true of getting online! I absolutely love this!"

And then I put some social media graphics together, like little pictures and words on them or comments and put those up. And she said, "Trish, I'm getting so many comments from friends and friends of friends about how much they love the social media posts! You are making this happen and this is so great! Thank you for taking this off of my shoulders!"

And it's so cool to see someone go from having all these amazing ideas in their head and on paper, pulling that out of them, and making it pretty and tying it up in a bow and then putting it out for the world to see. In this case, helping brides learn about a gown and how they can look their best and feel their best on their wedding day.

*How do you make sure the content marketing you provide is in your client's voice?*

**Tricia Prues:** One of the terms people will use is "ghostwriting," which sounds kind of weird. But we take someone's content and embrace their personality. Getting on a phone call with her initially was wonderful because I could really get a feel for her personality. And then we read some of the things that they've done and write as if we're putting ourselves in their shoes, so we are serving their audience in that way. And this particular client is super easy for me to write for because we get along very, very well.

Sometimes it's a good fit, sometimes it's not. And it's just finding people that you can really mesh with and understand their brain and their thinking, and then taking their brilliant ideas and running with them. It's not just making stuff up; it's taking this bit of information and then breaking it down and then putting it into something that will make it easy for people to consume it.

*Do people have to disclose whether their content is ghostwritten?*

**Tricia Prues:** Some people do. Some people do not want it disclosed that their work is ghostwritten, and other people go, "Well, it's fine. People still know that I'm serving them and providing quality content." Either way, you're embracing that person's voice, attitude, and personality. And it takes some research, too. But a lot of people go, "Great! You do this, take it, run with it." I mean, look at athletes who have books written. Michael

Jordan isn't sitting down writing a whole long book. He's doing what he does best and someone is writing the book and telling his story. And he doesn't have to be a writer. He does what he does best, and he has people who help him along the way with the things that he might not be best at. But he still has the wisdom and the knowledge and the experience to help people in other avenues.

*How did you get started with helping people with their content marketing and editing?*

**Tricia Prues:** Well, all my life, I was the "grammar wench," or whatever you want to call it. I loved writing. I was good at it. I loved helping people with their writing, and people would come to me saying, "Hey, will you help me with this piece or help me with my resume?" or, "Hey, I'm applying for a promotion at work. Will you help me with the essay?" Different things like that.

I found that people just were so relieved to get that help. But it was never a "thing" for me. I knew I was good at it, but I didn't really try to make a career out of it or anything, partially because I thought I would have to get an English degree and work at a newspaper. And the thought of that makes me want to barf. Newspaper people out there, I love you. That's great. That's just not my jam. And so, I went into another avenue.

I served in social work for a while, and then I was doing a little bit of life coaching when my friend Jennifer Harshman said, "You know, you really seem to have a knack for this editing thing." We were in a group coaching program together and I said, "Hey, do you think that this person would benefit from some editing on her pieces?" She said, "Yeah! Offer it!" And then she said, "You know what? I want you to take my editing test." It's kind of this test where you go through and edit a piece, then it's evaluated to see how it goes. And she said, "You are a natural-born editor! Why aren't you editing?" I said, "I don't know. I thought I had to work for a newspaper!" and she said, "No, you don't!" And she kind of took me under her wing.

It was so much fun, and I realized, "Yes, I can do this. I'm talented. I'm skilled. I'm experienced." Even though it's not something I'd put on a resume, I have helped people. People don't care what your credentials are. They want to know that you can help them with their problem. And I've helped people with their problem, and it's awesome.

And it's blossomed into not just editing a piece of a novel or editing a coaching manual and things like that. It's become, "How can you help me in these other areas?" And it happened pretty organically. I talked to someone about editing, she said, "And I'm thinking about doing this," and I said, "Well, I can help with that too!" Not to try and make myself a jack-of-all-trades, but I've learned these things, and in a lot of things out there, there's an aspect of editing, regardless of what it is.

If there's any written content that I'm helping you with, I'm not just going to take your stuff and put it out there. I'm going to read it, and I'm going to edit it if it needs to be edited. And it kind of just happened. It's just been really cool to see how people have been able to do their thing, and I can take the load off of their chest so they can focus on what they do best.

*What were your biggest challenges in starting to help people with their content marketing and editing?*

**Tricia Prues:** Sometimes I was afraid to ask for help because I didn't want to seem ignorant. Or I was afraid of saying, "Hey, I could use a little more time with this," because I want to please people. I want them to like my work, but I also don't want to compromise because I'm trying to be super efficient and awesome and amazing. I've learned, "Hey! Ask for an extended deadline." Most of the time people will give it to you.

And then, just being able to embrace me and know that people are going to understand what's going on. If they know that I care and I want to do a good job, and they want me to do a good job, we work together. So really, it's fears and insecurities of what people are going to think because I want to be great. And honestly, when people see you struggle and work through it and learn, they see greatness in that. Because they see a humility and an eagerness to better yourself and move along in your professional and personal growth.

*But people can be afraid of going back to ask for clarification, or ask for an extension because the client might act negatively. What do you recommend in those situations?*

**Tricia Prues:** Right. And if you do get a reaction like that, they might not be a good fit, so then just move on. But yeah, a lot of people, if their heart is in the right place, they want you to be transparent, and when you show that you want to fix something or do better in the future and are solution-focused, then they're probably going to want to stick with you because you're being authentic and transparent and genuine and caring.

*What is the most important question that business owners need to ask themselves before they jump into content marketing?*

**Tricia Prues:** "Am I ready to release this aspect of control? Am I ready to allow someone to come in and help?" I mean, let's be honest, I could really screw up a lot of people's lives because I have access to a lot of sensitive information. It's a matter of trust and finding someone who is trustworthy. I mean, I'm not going to sell your information. But you've gotta be ready to think about that. And you've got to say, "Am I ready to kind of release some of this control?" Because if you're not ready, you're going to have a really hard time connecting with someone and finding someone without always worrying.

*As they consider potential candidates to help with content marketing, what's the top thing they need to consider when making that choice?*

**Tricia Prues:** Personality. If two people don't mesh, it's not going to happen. And a great way to get a feel for that is getting on a phone call or a video chat because with written emails and things like that back and forth, it's just really hard to get a feel for someone's personality. But if you get on a call or video, you can get a feel for their personality.

If we go with our gut, and it's telling us it's just not going to work, then we kind of know. Or, "Oh my gosh, this is so great! I'm going to love working with this person!" And if there's some gray area, there's gray area, and we ask a few more questions and are able to kind of navigate what that looks like. But really, personality is bigger than skill. I mean, people can learn to do skills. You can't always teach someone character.

# About Tricia Prues

Tricia Prues helps coaches, consultants, and small-business owners use content marketing to attract more clients. She provides a wide range of services including ghostwriting, editing, content distribution, and website management.

**WEBSITE**
TriciaPrues.com

**EMAIL**
tricia@triciaprues.com

**LOCATION**
Cold Spring, KY

**FACEBOOK**
Facebook.com/TriciaPrues

# Fitness Over 40 Through Self Defense Training

If you're over 40 years of age and are experiencing significant changes in your body including increased weight and lower energy levels, you're not alone. Studies have shown that as we age we lose muscle and our metabolic rate decreases. Add to that the trends toward increasingly sedentary lifestyles, it's easy to understand how obesity rates have reached epidemic levels worldwide.

For older adults that are looking to maintain their physical health there is no lack of options. From yoga and Pilates, to fitness boot camps and high-intensity cross-training facilities, the sheer variety of available programs can be dizzying. But martial arts instructor and founder of Everyday Fighter Philipp Lomboy says that an ongoing self-defense training program can be the perfect fit.

In this interview, Philipp shares how a properly designed self-defense program can help adults improve their physical, mental, and emotional resilience well into the later years of their lives.

# Conversation with
# Philipp Lomboy of Everyday Fighter

*How would you describe your role as a self-defense instructor?*

**Philipp Lomboy:** I help students get a better sense of themselves and how to use their bodies through martial arts and self-defense techniques. While I have experience with all age groups, most of the students I teach are older, typically in their mid-thirties to late-forties and beyond.

The majority of older adults that I work with would not describe themselves as fighters or martial artists. In fact, many have never done any sort of martial arts prior to working with me. They're average people with regular day jobs, usually parents of school-age kids.

Through our curriculum our students are not only getting into better physical shape, but they're learning invaluable self-defense skills. That's the key difference of a self-defense program as compared to say a fitness boot camp - the exercises and movements we do on the mat can be used to help themselves stay safer should the unthinkable happen.

*What are the advantages of self-defense training for older adults?*

**Philipp Lomboy:** Variety is one of the biggest reasons our students come to us rather than to a gym or standard fitness bootcamp. They want to get into better shape but are looking for something other than cardio machines and weight training. There's absolutely nothing wrong with running or kettlebells - in fact, we incorporate those things into our self-defense program as well. But hitting a heavy bag till you're exhausted is a very different feeling. Throwing punches and kicks at a real person that's trying to do the same to you is a very different feeling.

A self-defense program also gives a unique context to the workout. In my classes I give specific scenarios that require focus, creativity, and physical exertion. It's not like doing rep after rep in a kind of hypnosis, which can be the case with many fitness-focused programs. The self-defense student really needs to be in tune to what's happening so that they can respond appropriately given the subtleties of a given scenario. Yes, they absolutely engage physically and get a good workout. But it also takes a good deal of mental and emotional control to handle these scenarios successfully.

For example, one of the scenarios we train involves someone attacking you from behind. Say an attacker "bear hugs" you from behind, trapping your arms to you your sides. It takes a great deal of physical exertion to handle that, but it also requires thought and adaptation on the fly. So, it'll take a few tries to get it right you're your partner. But then we tell them to find a new partner to work with, which can change the circumstances significantly - different height, weight, strength. So, you've got a good amount of variety built in to a specific context. You're not just mindlessly punching a bag.

And on top of all that, there's a very real emotional aspect they need to manage. Even in a training environment on a soft mat, it's never a pleasant experience to be suddenly grabbed from behind. Our philosophy is that the more we safely expose our students to feelings of shock and uncertainty, the better they'll be able to manage them if they experience it in a real threatening situation.

*What are some misconceptions around self-defense training, particularly for older adults?*

**Philipp Lomboy:** A very big misconception is the idea that training in self-defense means you can take on anybody at any time, like what they see in the movies. *The Karate Kid* or *The Matrix*, where ordinary people acquire a martial arts skill and can beat up multiple people at once, no matter their size, and walk away unscathed. It's romantic and exciting and, admittedly, the reason that many people get into martial arts and self-defense training. But it's a very dangerous notion.

The reality is that while you can learn self-defense skills, there are no guarantees. There are just too many variables that come into play - the physical environment, the size and skill of your attackers, whether you have children or other people with you, your state of mind.

We've all heard stories of trained professionals that froze and failed, when confronted with a real scenario, to perform their duties. These are people with dozens, if not hundreds, of hours of training. We've also heard of professionals that have performed in line with their training, but did not get their desired results. Maybe they bad guy got away, or they themselves were injured or worse.

But that fact that there are no guarantees is not a reason to avoid training. Every day we get into our automobiles and put on our seatbelts. If we get into a car accident, the seatbelt may or may not make a difference. But despite that reality, we still put on our seatbelts. We still teach our children to put on their seatbelts.

*What is a myth about self-defense?*

**Philipp Lomboy:** One of the mantras we've heard forever is that "knowledge is power." And while it is true to an extent, simply knowing techniques in your head doesn't mean you can apply them physically. You have to go beyond mental knowledge and get "hands-on" in order to experience any real benefits.

In our current environment of social media, clickbait, and easily-consumed content, a popular method for sharing self-defense "knowledge" is via short-form videos. In the video an "expert" describes a threatening situation and a self-defense technique to counter it. The underlying subtext in these videos is "if this happens, just do this and you'll be safe."

For now, I'll set aside the lack of dynamic movement and real resistance from the attacker. The bigger issue is that their approach relegates self-defense to a "factoid". The viewer feels like they've learned something, gets a rush of dopamine, and moves on. At the very least, this is disingenuous. At worst, it's irresponsible.

Another myth is that self-defense comes down to learning specific techniques. Yes, we teach techniques but those aren't the goal. The ultimate goal is to live your life happily and safely. Quite frankly I hope none of my students ever have to use the techniques that I teach them. I want them to experience joyous, happy, and long lives. For me a big part of that comes from improving their overall fitness.

There's a mantra that's used a lot nowadays in relation to active shooter situations: run, hide, fight. But the thing is, most people can barely run down the block without getting winded. So, in addition to techniques, I make sure to help improve my students' strength and endurance .

But even more importantly, having a better level of fitness staves off the bigger threats to a long and joyous life. Chronic illness, obesity, heart disease - statistically speaking these are much more likely to threaten the lives of my students than any criminal activity. If I can give them a good workout every time I see them, it improves their health and makes them better self-defenders.

*What are the common fears that keep older adults from starting self-defense program?*

**Philipp Lomboy:** A big fear is injuries. Either they have pre-existing injuries and don't want to make them worse, or they don't want to incur any injuries. We've all seen the warnings and disclaimers that you should talk to your doctor before starting any fitness program. A self-defense program is no different. This is absolutely the case if you're already injured. Neither my fellow instructors nor myself want to make things worse for any of our students. And while we want to train anyone that's willing to learn, we don't want to do that at the risk of increased injury. If it's an acute injury maybe it's a matter of waiting for it to heal before starting. If it's a chronic condition a doctor can advise the best course of action.

As far as getting injured, it's an absolute possibility - no different than running, biking, yoga, tennis, or any other form of physical activity. But rather than trying to avoid injuries, it may be better to consider ways to mitigate injury. Talk to the owner, instructor, and current students about appropriate protective gear and their gym's safety protocols. Have they worked with someone with your condition in the past? Would they be willing to modify their curriculum or teaching style to accommodate you? Will you still be able to benefit from the training given these modifications?

It's a very fine line we need to walk in all aspects of our lives - how to get the most out of our pursuits with as little risk as possible. Day traders use mathematical formulas and stop orders. Commercial truck drivers use multiple mirrors and defensive driving techniques. Self-defense students need to understand their physical limitations and how to work with them.

Another fear is setting foot in a self-defense school at all. It's a very vulnerable spot to be in at all. It feels like you're putting your future into someone else's hands. Couple that with violence (albeit controlled) and the risk of physical injury and it's no wonder many people feel intimidated to even open the door to a self-defense school. But many are able to start their journeys despite their fears by focusing instead on the benefits they'll enjoy - better health, variety, camaraderie, a new and exciting experience.

Technology can also help alleviate the feeling of intimidation. Social media, review sites, and YouTube have made easier than ever for the owners of self-defense programs to give potential students a preview of what they can expect beyond the front door of their school. So rather than relying on someone to walk through their front doors sight unseen, a student can get a good sense of the school's environment and approach well in advance. In fact, many students may have made their decision to join even before they set foot in the school.

*If they're able to get past these fears, what are some obstacles that can get in the way?*

**Philipp Lomboy:** As with most things, time and money are common obstacles for people that want to pursue self-defense training. To become proficient with self-defense skills, it's going to take a commitment of time and energy. Usually that means attending a 60-minute class at least twice per week. Fortunately, most schools have schedules that offer a variety of training times. For example, our school offers adult classes in the mornings and evenings Mondays through Saturday.

Ultimately, if you focus enough on the benefits you'll experience with self-defense training, it'll become a priority in your life. When that happens, you'll most likely find that other activities drop away and you have more than enough time to train.

Of course, good self-defense programs typically have a cost associated with them. But just as with time, once you see self-defense training as a priority, you'll probably find you have the funds to pursue it. Instead of seeing it as a "cost" or "expenditure" it'll be an "investment" in yourself and your family.

Another obstacle that keeps otherwise willing people from training in self-defense is location. They simply don't live in an area that a self-defense program close to them. As with most things, you just need to do the best that you can. When I was growing up there were many books and magazines from which I could get training in all manner of interests. Thanks to the Internet there are infinite resources available to help people that want to learn self-defense skills. More and more self-defense instructors are putting their curriculum online.

But there are two challenges with getting self-defense training online. The first is choice. The sheer volume of available programs can be dizzying. There are countless styles and just as many instructors in each. It can be challenging to decide where to start. The good news is that the investment in online courses can be a fraction of getting live, local training. And with lower price points, it's more feasible to try a wide variety of courses with very little risk.

The second challenge with online courses is a lack of actual, physical interaction, which is invaluable to learning self-defense. While drilling through shadow-boxing and bag work are integral parts of any program there is no substitute for training with a  live partner, ideally with multiple partners. Rather than one-sided exercises on your own, partners give you a dynamic, varied training experience. This will also make you a better self-defender. If you don't have a training facility nearby, you might consider recruiting like-minded friends and family to work with you through the online course. You might also consider traveling occasionally to attend in-person training seminars and workshops in other cities.

In the end, when it comes to time, money, and access, we can only do the best with what we've got. But you also have to be honest about your level of skill and competency.

*What are some common mistakes that new self-defense students make?*

**Philipp Lomboy:** One mistake is choosing a program based solely on location. Having a program with a convenient location is a big factor for actually showing up to classes. We've all had those days where we're just exhausted from work and decide to skip a workout because the drive was too far.

If the school was closer we'd miss fewer workouts. But just because your school is easy to get to doesn't mean that you'll go. If you're not getting quality instruction and you're not enjoying your training, there's little chance that you'll show up even if your school is next door.

In addition to location, here are few things to consider when deciding on the right self-defense program for you:

- Does their class schedule work with your calendar?
- What's their approach to self-defense and is it in line with what you're looking for?
- Is the school clean and well equipped?
- Do you get along with the other students?
- How do you feel about your instructor's teaching style?
- Do they train with other schools?

Even if after you decide on a school, nothing says you have to stay there forever. You may find that your initial impression was wrong. Maybe the program or climate of the school changed over time. Maybe you made it all the way through their entire program.

In those cases, it may make sense to move on to a different school. And nothing says you can't attend multiple schools and programs concurrently. If that's a priority in your life and you have the time and resources, why not?

*How long can someone train in self-defense?*

**Philipp Lomboy:** Self-defense training isn't relegated to specific age groups. There are programs for children as young as 5 years old to adults of all ages.

One of my regular students is a retired gentleman, 65 years old. He is also a youth basketball referee for our local high schools. In his thirties, he started training in a traditional martial arts style and achieved his 2nd degree black belt. After taking a break he decided that he wanted to train Krav Maga and self-defense. That's how he found our school. He has some minor limits on his mobility so he makes adjustments as necessary. But aside from that he works through our curriculum and sparring sessions very well.

A few months after training with us he pulled me aside and said, "This program has really helped me when I referee my basketball games. I even do the same warmups on the court that we do here on the mat. I have so much more energy now and I barely break a sweat as I run up and down the court after these teenagers." He went on to say that his fellow referees had mentioned difference in him as well.

Another student is a sports therapist, coaches girls volleyball, and is 76 years old. Rather than going to our group classes, he gets private lessons from our other instructors at our school.

You can do self-defense training for as long as you and your body are willing.

Here's an even bigger consideration. The average person's activity level decreases significantly as they get older. Their mobility, strength, and energy levels are much lower, which means they're much more vulnerable to attack. Predators and criminals generally don't want to approach people that are strong and fit and more likely to fight back.

But an elderly person with diminished physical capacity is a much easier target. By training in self-defense as you get older, not only will you retain your physical abilities to better enjoy your life, you'll potentially avoid having to use your self-defense skills altogether because you're less likely to be approached as a victim.

*How did you get started down the road to self-defense?*

**Philipp Lomboy:** I started traditional martial arts in my early twenties. I had always wanted to learn, but didn't get the chance to do it till I had a job and was living on my own. I started training in traditional karate, but I didn't realize until much later that what I was learning was very different from "real" self-defense.

Many martial arts schools automatically add "self-defense" to their signs and brochures. The general feeling is that if you're punching, kicking, or otherwise training to hit others, that qualifies as self-defense. And while that can technically be the case, it's far from reality. But again, at the time I didn't know any different.

It wasn't until I was introduced to Krav Maga that I discovered another point of view where self-defense went well beyond a series of choreographed attacks and movements.

I learned that self-defense was better approached with general principles rather than detailed responses to specific scenarios. I learned that it was chaotic, dynamic, violent, emotional, and exhausting.

While a small part of me was frustrated that wasn't taught those realities in the past, a bigger part of me was intrigued and excited by the possibilities and real life application of the new concepts I was learning.

Even as an instructor myself, I learn something new every day. I learn just as much from my students as I do other self-defense instructors, which is why I'm confident that I'll continue training well into the later years of my life.

Beyond my personal growth, I think self-defense is an important thing for anyone to learn. Just like we go to school to learn how to read and write, we should also learn how to defend ourselves. While we can do everything we can to live good lives as law-abiding citizens, there's always a chance we'll run into someone that doesn't follow the same rules.

With that in mind, I think you're much better off knowing how to protect yourself and your family members. As they say, hope for the best, but prepare for the worst. Again, it's just like knowing how to buckle your seatbelt in your car.

Also, as the father of four daughters I am acutely aware that I cannot be there to protect them at every step in their lives. I also know that trying to do that wouldn't serve them or me. It would be better for me to teach them how to defend themselves.

And that doesn't just mean protecting themselves from bogeymen in hoodies or overeager boyfriends. Hands on self-defense skills are just a part of a bigger umbrella of self-protection and self-care that includes effective communication skills, conflict avoidance, and setting proper boundaries.

*As older adults consider taking a self-defense program, what's the most important question they should ask themselves?*

**Philipp Lomboy:** "What do I have to lose?" Honestly, I don't think there are many downsides to training in self defense. Just like lifting weights doesn't mean you're thinking about being a bodybuilder, training in self defense doesn't mean you're paranoid about being attacked by someone. Again, I have nothing against any other form of fitness. But self-defense training has the inherent benefit of usability.

*What's the most important question people should consider when choosing a self-defense school and instructor?*

**Philipp Lomboy:** "Is this person an active student themselves?" Things change in our society all the time, and nothing is immune to that. A hundred years ago we couldn't imagine the types of personal and societal threats that are possible today. "Active shooter" is unfortunately now a part of our everyday language. While we don't want to be paranoid about those things happening to us, we need to be prepared.

A good self-defense program needs to adapt their curriculum and teaching styles accordingly. If an instructor just teaches the same thing year after year, decade after decade, that tells me that they aren't adapting with the times and aren't interested in the continued growth of their students. I don't think it means that the school has to teach everything under the sun, but there has to come a point where they are honest about what they're teaching, and make appropriate changes over time.

# About Philipp Lomboy

Philipp Lomboy is a martial arts and self-defense instructor in Southern California. He is the founder of Everyday Fighter which provides online martial arts and self-defense instruction. Philipp also hosts the Everyday Fighter podcast where he shares stories and insights from people with a passion for the fight world.

**WEBSITE**
EverydayFighter.me

**FACEBOOK**
Facebook.com/EverydayFighter.me

**INSTAGRAM**
Instagram.com/EverydayFighter.me

# Thriving in Retirement Without Outliving Your Income – Critical Factors in Choosing a Financial Planner and Wealth Manager You Can Trust

Matthew Unger created Focus Asset Management to deliver an unsurpassed experience to affluent and high net worth individuals, their families, foundations and businesses. By providing advice founded on a culture of excellence and driven by global insight, Focus delivers this within the context of an unparalleled, elite and independent registered investment advisory firm, not unlike an independent family office.

Focus Asset Management Managing Director and Senior Advisor, Matthew Unger Discusses His Approach to Helping His Clients with Financial Planning and Wealth Management

# Conversation with Matthew Unger

*Tell us about Focus Asset Management how you help your clients?*

**Matthew Unger:** Sure. We are a boutique financial advisory firm that specializes in two areas. One is financial planning and then two, is the investment management of their assets. What we look to do is provide a high-touch, high-quality service to individuals that typically have half a million in assets and up from there.

*What do you do to show people what your recommended plan is for them?*

**Matthew Unger:** Really what we look to do is understand our clients, really in two areas. We want to understand them qualitatively and quantitatively. We're going to pop the hood in the first meeting or two that we have together. I really want to get to know the individual and what makes them tick, because at the end of the day, if we're going to manage their assets, we're not going to be able to implement a plan that will bring them the success that they're looking for if we don't know them as individuals.

For example, someone coming to us that has minimal cash-flow needs and maybe, let's say $600,000 investible assets, we'll have a far different plan than somebody who has a one and a half million-dollar estate planning need for example, or other complicated issues.

We look to make a bespoke and customizable experience for each one of our clients, and we also do that by keeping our client rosters smaller. Typically, some of the larger firms you'll hear of, you'll have 300-500 clients on an advisors' roster, and there have been studies that show humans can only deal with about 150 relationships, and our advisors that we will have, and specifically me to start, will have about half that roster size.

*Let's talk a little bit more about high touch. What does that look like and what are some expectations that your clients should come to expect?*

**Matthew Unger:** Assuming you're not emailing on a Friday night, or on a holiday weekday, you can expect to get a response at the latest, either by the end of the business day or within 24 hours, depending on the complexity of the issue. What most clients find when they're with me, sometimes I may come across as that overbearing mother a little bit. I'd rather my clients be annoyed by me contacting them too much versus them not hearing from me enough.

Really what you hear in the financial services industry, you get this slick talking guy, he's got a really nice suit on, a bunch of nice looking cuff links and shiny shoes, that'll come to your house and take your $1,000,000 under management and after the first three or four meetings you never really hear from them again. What we pride ourselves on at Focus is not only gaining your trust and your respect, to begin up front, we also want to educate you.

We want you to understand what is happening with your money and additionally, I want to add, we have some clients that may not want us to manage their assets, but they want us for advice. So that's where that financial planning comes in. A lot of firms simply won't give you advice unless they have your assets. We don't necessarily need to have your assets at Focus to give you genuine, customized, specialized advice.

*That's a significant distinction because how advisors these days typically get paid is "Assets Under Management." You speak and teach about helping your clients not outlive their income. What are the advantages of focusing on that, not outliving your income?*

**Matthew Unger:** I'd like to say upfront; we do not sell annuities. A lot of the time you'll hear people say, "oh you want guaranteed lifetime income, here let's talk about this investment vehicle," and it turns out to be a very expensive annuity.

We don't think annuities are bad. In fact, in some instances, they work very well for clients. What we find more often than not, what clients genuinely care about is the money that they have worked their entire life saving, sacrificing, blood, sweat, and tears, you name it. They want to know, not only is that going to be okay for when they need it, but they also want to make sure that they're not spending it all in 10 years.

I mean a lot of folks know one person in their network that had a great retirement for 10, 15 years and suddenly, they're 80, 85, 90, but they only expected to live until their late 70s or early 80s. With life expectancy tables moving out further and further every year it seems, clients are struggling not only in managing their cash-flows, but also understanding where to put their assets.

*What do you feel are some misconceptions that people have around, even just the investment and financial planning industry, but primarily related to outliving their income?*

**Matthew Unger:**   Well, there are a lot of them; one that I come across over and repeatedly is fear of failure. This backs people into a corner, and sometimes they get stuck permanently and fail to plan.

Clients often believe every investment they have in their portfolio needs to work and they define the success of an investment by its performance and often they make the mistake of, well I've had XYZ company in my portfolio, it's performed terribly -20% for the last year or two and they go sell it. Well, what are they doing? They're doing the opposite of the cardinal rule of "buy low, sell high."

They're buying high and selling low. What I help my clients understand is how to get into, what I call the ready-to-fail mindset and now while that might sound a little negative, when you have a lot of little things that you have going at once, for example, a variety of positions in a portfolio, be ready for some of those to fail. But what people fail to realize, typically in portfolio management is that your big winners offset your big losers.

The bulk of the return in your portfolio comes from the middle of the portfolio, the ones that are performing five, six, seven, eight percent a year. Having a client understand there are certain risks associated with how they manage their portfolio, such as bonds carry more volatility risk overtime because they're actually more volatile than stocks in the long run. I have this conversation with my clients quite frequently actually. So, if you have a couple of components in a portfolio that are "failing," that are not doing well, well if it's appropriately diversified, that's okay. What I find clients hire me for is for me to worry about that.

They want to go off and see their grandchildren. They want to go to the movies. They want to be able to go to graduation parties. They want to buy a boat maybe and enjoy life on the ocean. Well, I ask clients, especially in down-markets, did they picture watching CNBC every day and panicking when the market goes down? Is that how they imagined their retirement? Or did they picture enjoying time with their grandkids? They want to be enjoying time out playing golf and doing other activities that they love! I help clients identify the areas that they wish to enjoy in their life, and then I take care of the how.

They're at point A; they want to get to point B. I specialize in creating that plan for them.

*Do you feel like also a misconception could be that there will be fluctuations to the plan? Talk a little bit about that misconception of how this plan is accurate, but there could be some ebbs and flows that are all part of the process.*

**Matthew Unger:**   Yeah and I call that the "number factor misconception" and what I mean by that is you'll look at the retirement marketing today and commercials on TV and what do they say? "What's your number?"

You see these people walking around holding their numbers. One person has 1.4 million; the other one has 2.6 million. That marketing generates an image in one's mind that they need X amount of dollars to retire. What do they need their number to be? What the marketing was meant to show was, this is the dollar amount you need throughout retirement. A lot of people have a hard time understanding, "Matt, I brought you a portfolio of $500,000 when we started, 15 years later it's still $500,000. You're getting me a zero percent return." I come back and say, well, you know Mr. and Mrs. client, don't forget you've been taking about $40,000 a year from your portfolio, through the ups and downs.

Over time, what clients can sometimes forget is I just took out $400,000 from this account over the last 12 to 15 years, but I still have half a million left over. Oh, and by the way, I still have 15 years to go! Again, remember we talked about life expectancy going further out on the tables, and suddenly it's not all about performance. What I show my clients, and where I shine for them, is this: What if you had $20,000, for example, but you can turn that $20,000 into the income that you needed? It doesn't matter what you end up with, and then you have the "neighbor syndrome," (my neighbor has this amount, and they're doing this, and their return was that).

What I often find out is, they'll sometimes even refer the neighbors to me, because the neighbors have just been lying. What I find specifically about my clients is they are often the person in the room with the most money, and they don't realize it.

They're the ones sitting on, and their neighbors might just be talking up ... it may be true, they may have wealthy and other affluent friends, but I find my clients, typically the millionaire next door, who's worked hard their entire life, saved almost every penny they possibly could, they don't consider themselves to be rich -

But what they don't tend to realize is that they're the wealthiest person in the room.

*Do you feel like sometimes people are making a comparison incorrectly?*

**Matthew Unger:** Right. I call that "benchmarking bias."

Sal the neighbor who's also a fisherman like me is doing this much in retirement. I'm only taking in $50,000 in income; he's taking in a $100,000.

What you don't know is Sal is on a depletionary trajectory, and he's going to run out of money in five years.

Sal might be running up his credit cards personally and needing to take all that out to pay his credit cards, and you're not. There's a lot of variables.

I don't mean to generalize here, but often my clients find out quickly that not only are they usually savvier than the people that they're trying to keep up with, but they're also generally in a much better situation than they are.

Crossing goals with someone else can be very dangerous. If you're chasing return, "oh, my buddy got 26% last year, my portfolio only did 15%," well, again, performance is part of it, but if it's getting you to your objective and where you need to go, it doesn't matter you know.

If you're making a cross country trip, you're probably going to spend most of your time in the left lane, right? Unless you're like me and you're afraid of highways, and you drive 60 in the right lane the entire time. But, if you're plan dictates that you need to be in the far-left lane, it's where you need to be. We run a statistical probability analysis to decide where our clients need to be invested, because we have to worry about supporting their cash flows. More importantly, we have to support those cash flows throughout their longevity, which often tends to be much longer than they initially expected.

*Matthew, can you think of an example of some time that you worked with a client to help them not outlive their income, and you put a plan into action and the result that they're experiencing?*

**Matthew Unger:** Absolutely. I'll never forget one client, back in 2018, he kept going to cash because he was really worried about the volatility in the market.

I said, let's do an analysis. Do you need to be in the market anymore? He was in his late 70s, he had multiple income sources, not just the portfolio that I had and I sat down with him and educated him on how he needs to help kind of lock down his behavior when markets get jittery and shut of CNBC and spend some more time with grandkids and he started doing that. As soon as he started doing that, my call volume with him dropped precipitously.

Now I enjoy talking to him, so I'm not bragging that he stopped calling me by any means.

Often the markets don't do investors in; investors do themselves in. I may be misquoting Warren Buffett, but that's a Warren Buffett quote. Another one is markets are a very efficient mechanism to transfer wealth from the impatient to the patient. What this client finally realized was that going in and out of the market was costing him, not just thousands of dollars in the interim, but hundreds of thousands of dollars down the line when you consider compounding.

*What was your initial inspiration to become a wealth manager?*

**Matthew Unger:** Unfortunately, I abandoned those dreams of firefighter and pilot probably around age three, but they've always kind of stuck with me on the side. All seriousness, I had a very, very close member of my family almost goes bankrupt and will never forget, while sitting on the stoop at my apartment complex in New York City when I got the call, and they said that they might be going bankrupt. At that moment, I realized how critical financial literacy is for every individual and not only just the importance of financial literacy but also understanding how finance is life. I think Chase Manhattan has the saying, "so you can." I think that's brilliant.

You don't save money up so that you can beat and pound your chest and dive into a pool of gold coins like Scrooge McDuck did and, well, maybe that is your goal.

In all seriousness, most individuals want to save and use their portfolio, whether it's invested or not, to support their lifestyle.

"So, you can," right? It comes back to that saying. That moment was life changing for me and hearing this family member was almost going bankrupt, and I decided to devote the rest of my life's work to prevent that happening to as many families as possible. That's why I became an advisor.

*What was the lesson you learned, even from that, that still impacts you today on how you advise your clients from that experience, what was maybe one of the main lessons you pulled away from that?*

**Matthew Unger:** I would say "never sugarcoat," and I mean that in how I treat my clients, but I also expect that out of my clients and how they handle themselves. If there's a problem, speak up about it. You've got to address it. I'll help you address it, and sometimes I'll spot a problem before a client does. If you gloss over that problem and sugarcoat it, well are you ever really going to get to the problem? I think there's a famous saying, "to improve yourself or to solve a problem, one must admit they have one in the first place."

That can be very difficult, and in a society where talking about finances is taboo in public with your friends you don't go around saying, oh I get paid this, so I have this in savings. We're a very private society in that sense. What is so important for clients and even for me, is never to sugarcoat and I tell you, it's tough. It is tough having a conversation with a 72-year-old who thinks they are set but are on a tremendous depletionary trajectory and it's usually not because they're going out and gambling it all away. It's the death by a thousand cuts.

The air conditioner goes out here; the roof needs replacing, their child falls sick; $10,000 hospital bill. You need a hip replaced, that's a lot more than $10,000. Retirement's not linear and so admitting to problems along the way is one thing, but making adjustments is as equally important as acknowledging that there is a problem by not sugarcoating, right? We can't control the wind, but we can adjust our sails, and that's what a good advisor does, and a good client follows suit and both admit when there's an issue.

*What do you feel are some of the most critical questions that they should be asking themselves and considering?*

**Matthew Unger:** I would say it's a two-part question. It's usually one question that leads to the other. Which is, what do I want my retirement to look like? Do you know you are going to be traveling more? Are you going to want to relocate to be closer to the family? Do you want to transfer to a facility that maybe offers better medical services? Right. That usually then leads to how much money do I need in retirement? I think that's probably the golden question and that you can, you really can't put a number on that like the way the marketing does.

Because it's different for everyone. Think about this; let's say everybody needed 2,000,000 to retire; let's say that society was precisely the same.

Well, what happens when one family goes through a car accident?

Their needs change drastically in an instant.

Which may or may not mean you need to make a significant change. I mean I had a client who had to reinstall their entire gas line in California, it was going to cost them $20,000 up front and $20,000 on job completion. It was damage caused by the Candlestick Park earthquake out in San Fran decades ago. I also had a client that lived not far from them, they knew each other, and they had about the same dollar amount. This client called panicking; we're going to run out of money, $40,000, this is a disaster.

I ran a scenario for them, I did a stress test for their portfolio, and I said, you're fine. It's going to be okay. A lot of clients, when tragedy strikes, whatever that means to them, sometimes it's not as bad as they think it is.

Having someone there, like an advisor to kind of double check it for you is so important. If you're not feeling well, you probably should go to the doctor. Also, possibly consider getting a second opinion as well.

*What would be the best way that someone could reach out and connect with you and maybe get that second opinion?*

**Matthew Unger:** Our website is very user-friendly. It's www.FocusAssetMgmt.com

On our site, we have a free crash course video on the three vital elements to early retirement. What I like about this video is, it touches on things that are important to those that are looking to retire. Whether it's early or not, this video happens to be on early retirement. Then there's another video that reviews the consequences of waiting to plan for retirement. It's a small case study that we do. That's a great way to learn more about how we serve our clients.

# About Matthew Unger

Prior to forming Focus Asset Management, Matthew was an advisor with Fisher Investments where he was responsible for managing approximately $150 million in assets, where he signed $35 million in new client assets in 2018, Ranked in the Top 1% for new client on-boarding and retention for Fiscal Year 2018 and constantly lead his team in client satisfaction.

Matthew also previously worked at Merrill Lynch, Pierce Fenner & Smith where he advised affluent individuals and families.

Matthew attended Syracuse University for under-graduate, and Harvard University for graduate work, and obtained a Professional Certificate in Financial Markets from Yale University.

Matthew has 12+ years of professional experience, and 10 years of investment advisory and consulting experience.

**WEBSITE**

www.FocusAssetMgmt.com

www.ingramcontent.com/pod-product-compliance
Lightning Source LLC
Chambersburg PA
CBHW071110210326
41519CB00020B/6249